Elephant's Guide to Making Friends

Published in 2026 by Windmill Books,
an Imprint of Rosen Publishing
2544 Clinton St.
Buffalo, NY 14224

First published in Great Britain in 2023 in 2023 by Hodder & Stoughton

Credits
Commissioning editor: Sarah Peutrill
Series editor: Lisa Edwards
Series Designer: Rachel Lawston

Cataloging-in-Publication Data

Names: Edwards, Lisa, author. | Roberts, Sian, illustrator.
Title: Elephant's guide to making friends / Lisa Edwards, illustrated by Sian Roberts.
Description: Buffalo, NY : Windmill Books, 2026. | Series: Healthy habits
Identifiers: ISBN 9781538399521 (pbk.) | ISBN 9781538399538 (library bound) | ISBN 9781538399545 (ebook)
Subjects: LCSH: Friendship--Juvenile literature. | Interpersonal relations--Juvenile literature. | Elephants--Juvenile literature.
Classification: LCC BF723.F68 E393 2026 | DDC 177'.62--dc2

Printed in the United States of America

CPSIA Compliance Information: Batch #CSWM26
For Further Information contact Rosen Publishing at 1-800-237-9932

Healthy Habits

Elephant's Guide to Making Friends

Lisa Edwards

Siân Roberts

WINDMILL BOOKS

Elephant and his mom are going to the waterhole for a morning drink. Grandma is leading the way.

Elephant lives in a herd with lots of other young elephants, called calves.

Elephant's friends say good morning with their trunks!

Elephant loves to play at the waterhole. He uses his trunk to spray water over himself and his friends.

He also loves to splash around and cover himself in mud. It's fun to play with your friends!

One of Elephant's friends has hurt her leg!

He comforts his friend using his trunk, while Grandma helps her to stand up again.

A good friend always makes sure that their friend is OK if they're sick or upset.

Elephant is having his breakfast. He browses for good things to eat: grasses, small plants, bushes, fruit, twigs, tree bark, and roots.

Elephant shows his friends where to find the best food.
Friends help each other and share what they have.

Grandma always remembers the best places to find water for her herd. Like all elephants, she has a very good memory.

Remembering a friend's birthday is important.
How do you like to celebrate yours?

Elephant sees his friend in another herd.
He wraps his trunk around her, clicks his tusks,
and flaps his ears in excitement!

It's important to make your friends feel loved and valued. A smile or a hug are good ways to do that.

Elephant learns that his friend is feeling sad. She has become separated from her mother.

Elephant listens to his friend and comforts her. When your friend is upset, you can listen and offer to help them.

Elephant tells his grandma about his friend's problem. She welcomes the other herd to join hers, so they can all look after each other.

It's important to make sure friends feel supported. Remember to make sure no one feels left out of a group.

The next morning, one of the calves is unhappy with the new herd. He gets angry, flapping his ears and trumpeting very loudly!

Elephant talks to the unhappy calf, helping him to understand why the new elephants have joined them. Being open to new people and understanding how they live is important.

The calf says sorry for being angry and
they all make up.

Always say sorry if you upset someone. You should also try to forgive someone when they say sorry to you.

Grandma meets the head of the new herd and they decide which of them will lead everyone to their next feeding ground. Elephant's grandma is the oldest so she will do it.

Working together for the good of everyone around you is always the best way.

When Elephant talks to his friends, he makes very low sounds that we cannot hear, called infrasound.

Your friends are people you can talk to about anything and everything. But always remember to use kind words and listen too!

Elephant has been showing us how he makes friends. How can you make friends?

Spend time with people you like

Have fun with your friends

Be kind to your friends

Help your friends and share what you have

Make your friends feel loved and valued

Support your friends and help them

See things from your friends' side

Say sorry when you upset your friends
(and forgive them if they upset you)

Think about what is best for your friends, not just yourself

Listen and talk to your friends

Glossary

Browse to feed on leaves and twigs, mostly high up on trees and bushes.

Calves the name given to baby elephants.

Celebrate to mark an important day with activities such as eating special food.

Comfort to make someone feel better with kind words or a hug.

Feeding ground an area where wild animals like to eat.

Herd the name given to a large group of animals who live together.

Infrasound a sound that is unable to be heard by human ears.

Memories things that are remembered from the past.

Support to help someone, especially if they are having a difficult time.

Trunk the long nose of an elephant.

Trumpet the sound an elephant makes with its trunk.

Tusks the teeth of an elephant, growing on either side of their mouths.

Waterhole a dip in the ground in which water collects, where animals drink.

Let's talk about healthy habits...

The *Healthy Habits* series has been written to help young children begin to understand how they can live healthy lives, both in their relationships with others and in their own bodies.

It provides a starting point for parents, caregivers, and teachers to discuss healthy ways of being in the world with little learners. The series involves a cast of animal characters who behave in healthy ways in their own habitats, relating their experiences to familiar, everyday scenarios for children.

Elephant's Guide to Making Friends

This story looks at all the ways you can make friends.
The book aims to encourage a child's sense of empathy and its importance, along with kindness, in relationships with others. It offers children a simple checklist that they can use to remember what is important in their existing and future friendships.

How to use the book:

The book is designed for adults to share with either an individual child, or a group of children, and as a starting point for discussion.

Choose a time when you and the children are relaxed and have time to share the story.

Before reading the story:

- Spend time looking at the illustrations and talking about what the book might be about before reading it together. Ask the children to look at the details in each picture to see what all the creatures are doing – some of them are echoing the main themes in the background of the story.

- Encourage children to employ a "phonics-first" approach to tackling new words by sounding them out.

After reading the story:

- Talk about the story with the children. Ask the children to list the best things about being with their friends.
- Ask them to think about occasions when a friend has made them feel happy. What specific things did they do?
- Place the children into groups and ask them to imagine it's a friend's birthday in a week's time. What things should they think about doing to show their friend how important they are to them?
- At the end of the session, discuss what makes a healthy friendship with the whole class and list all the ways we can support our friends if they have a problem. Finish by talking about how sharing and being kind to your friends can make you feel good too.